Old English Trumpet Tunes

Alte Englische Trompetenmelodien

PREFACE

The trumpet enjoys a popularity today probably not exceeded in any other period of its long history as a solo instrument. During the 17th and early 18th centuries it was accorded special treatment by composers such as Purcell, Handel and Bach, and given solo obbligato passages of arresting beauty in instrumental and vocal works. With the long narrow-bore instrument in D, the player was able to negotiate complex and high-lying melodic passages without the aid of valves. Many 'trumpet' tunes were written for the harpsichord and organ by eminent English composers of the 17th century such as Purcell, Clarke and Croft under the influence of Shore, the famous trumpeter to the court of Queen Anne, and subsequent writers such as Boyce and Greene carried on the tradition.

S.M.L.

VORWORT

Die Trompete ist heute so beliebt, wie sie es wahrscheinlich noch nie zuvor in ihrer langen Geschichte als Soloinstrument war. Im 17. und 18. Jahrhundert genoss sie durch Komponisten wie Purcell, Händel und Bach eine Sonderbehandlung, und sowohl in Instrumental- als auch in Vokalwerken wurden ihr hauptstimmige Solopassagen von erhebender Schönheit zugedacht. Mit dem langen, engröhrigen Instrument in D konnten schwierige, hochliegende melodische Passagen ohne Ventile gespielt werden. Unter dem Einfluss von Shore, dem berühmten Trompeter am Hof von Königin Anne, schrieben bedeutende Komponisten des 17. Jahrhunderts, wie Purcell, Clarke und Croft, viele "Trompetenmelodien", und von späteren Komponisten wie Boyce und Greene wurde diese Tradition fortgesetzt.

S.M.L.

CONTENTS

Old English Trumpet Tunes Book 2
is also available.

OLD ENGLISH TRUMPET TUNES

1
TRUMPET TUNE
(from "The Indian Queen" Act II)

HENRY PURCELL
(1659-1695)

2
TRUMPET AIR

(from the Additional Act to "The Indian Queen")

DANIEL PURCELL
(c. 1660-1717)

Daniel Purcell was a younger brother of Henry Purcell. From 1688-1695 he was organist of
Magdalen College Oxford. He then returned to London and became a popular composer for the theatre.

Old English Trumpet Tunes

3
MARCH

(from "Scipio" Act I)

HANDEL
(1685-1759)

Old English Trumpet Tunes

4
MARCH
(from the Overture to the Occasional Oratorio)

HANDEL

This arrangement has been made from the Wright and Arnold full scores by kind permission of the Syndics of the Fitzwilliam Museum, Cambridge

Old English Trumpet Tunes

Old English Trumpet Tunes

5
TRUMPET TUNE, CALLED THE CEBELL

HENRY PURCELL

★ Alternative reading

Old English Trumpet Tunes

6
MINUET AND TRIO

(from the Music for the Royal Fireworks)

HANDEL

Old English Trumpet Tunes

7
A TRUMPET MINUET

JEREMIAH CLARKE
(c. 1673-1707)

★ Notes in small type are optional

Old English Trumpet Tunes

Old English Trumpet Tunes

8
TRUMPET TUNE

HENRY PURCELL

Allegro moderato

Old English Trumpet Tunes

Oxford University Press

OLD ENGLISH TRUMPET TUNES

1
TRUMPET TUNE

(from "The Indian Queen" Act II)

HENRY PURCELL
(1659-1695)

2
TRUMPET AIR

(from the Additional Act to "The Indian Queen")

DANIEL PURCELL
(c. 1660-1717)

Daniel Purcell was a younger brother of Henry Purcell. From 1688-1695 he was organist of Magdalen College Oxford. He then returned to London and became a popular composer for the theatre.

3
MARCH

(from "Scipio" Act I)

HANDEL
(1685-1759)

4
MARCH
(from the Overture to the Occasional Oratorio)

HANDEL

5
TRUMPET TUNE, CALLED THE CEBELL

HENRY PURCELL

Old English Trumpet Tunes

★ Alternative reading

6
MINUET AND TRIO
(from the Music for the Royal Fireworks)

HANDEL

Pomposo

last time rall.   *Fine*   Minuet D.C.

7
A TRUMPET MINUET

JEREMIAH CLARKE
(c. 1673-1707)

8
TRUMPET TUNE

HENRY PURCELL

Old English Trumpet Tunes

9
THE PRINCE OF DENMARK'S MARCH

JEREMIAH CLARKE
(c. 1673-1707)

10
TRUMPET TUNE

MAURICE GREENE
(1695-1755)

11
TRUMPET VOLUNTARY

JOHN STANLEY (1713–1786)
Op. 6 No. 5

Andante Largo

Although Stanley's 'Andante Largo' indicates a stately tempo, the style should be pointed and rhythmic. When not slurred, the figure should be interpreted

12
1st Movement from the
SONATA FOR TRUMPET AND STRINGS

HENRY PURCELL
(1659 – 1695)

This transcription has been made from an early 18th. century MS. in the
library of York Minster, by kind permission of the Dean and Chapter.

13
TRUMPET VOLUNTARY

WILLIAM BOYCE
(1710-1779)

Old English Trumpet Tunes

Old English Trumpet Tunes

9
THE PRINCE OF DENMARK'S MARCH

JEREMIAH CLARKE
(c. 1673-1707)

Old English Trumpet Tunes

Old English Trumpet Tunes

10
TRUMPET TUNE

MAURICE GREENE
(1695-1755)

Old English Trumpet Tunes

18

Old English Trumpet Tunes

11
TRUMPET VOLUNTARY

JOHN STANLEY (1713–1786)
Op. 6 No. 5

Although Stanley's 'Andante Largo' indicates a stately tempo, the style should be pointed and rhythmic. When not slurred, the ♩♪ figure should be interpreted ♩ 𝄽♪

Old English Trumpet Tunes

Old English Trumpet Tunes

Old English Trumpet Tunes

12
1st Movement from the
SONATA FOR TRUMPET AND STRINGS

HENRY PURCELL
(1659 – 1695)

This transcription has been made from an early 18th. century MS. in the
library of York Minster, by kind permission of the Dean and Chapter.

Old English Trumpet Tunes

Old English Trumpet Tunes

24

Old English Trumpet Tunes

13
TRUMPET VOLUNTARY

WILLIAM BOYCE
(1710-1779)

Old English Trumpet Tunes

Old English Trumpet Tunes

Old English Trumpet Tunes

Processed and printed by
Halstan & Co. Ltd., Amersham, Bucks., England

OXFORD UNIVERSITY PRESS